Summary

Awaken the Giant Within

How to Take Immediate Control of Your Mental, Emotional, Physical & Financial Destiny!

by Tony Robbins

Instaread

Please Note

This is a summary with analysis.

Copyright © 2016 by Instaread. All rights reserved worldwide. No part of this publication may be reproduced or transmitted in any form without the prior written consent of the publisher.

Limit of Liability/Disclaimer of Warranty: The publisher and author make no representations or warranties with respect to the accuracy or completeness of these contents and disclaim all warranties such as warranties of fitness for a particular purpose. The author or publisher is not liable for any damages whatsoever. The fact that an individual or organization is referred to in this document as a citation or source of information does not imply that the author or publisher endorses the information that the individual or organization provided. This concise summary is unofficial and is not authorized, approved, licensed, or endorsed by the original book's author or publisher.

Table of Contents

Overview 5

Important People 7

Key Takeaways 8

Analysis 11

Key Takeaway 1 11

Key Takeaway 2 13

Key Takeaway 3 15

Key Takeaway 4 16

Key Takeaway 5 17

Key Takeaway 6 19

Key Takeaway 7 20

Key Takeaway 8 21

Key Takeaway 9 23

Key Takeaway 10 24

Key Takeaway 11 26

Author's Style 27

Author's Perspective 28

References 30

Overview

Awaken the Giant Within by motivational speaker Tony Robbins is a comprehensive self-help book designed for people who want to feel in control of all aspects of their lives and fulfill their greatest potential in their relationships, career, finances, and personal lives.

Everyone is born with the capacity to be happy and achieve their greatest destiny, but not everyone is happy and fulfilled. To illustrate the powerful lessons he's learned about success, personal growth, and transformation, Robbins taps into his years of experience as a personal and professional coach, his own experience in surmounting obstacles and thriving, and anecdotes about high-achieving people. He indicates that these lessons are available for anyone to apply regardless of background or past failures.

At one time or another, everyone has had a glimpse of their best life, or who they think they could become in an ideal world. Sustaining the motivation to make those dreams a reality can be daunting in the face of everyday responsibilities. Over time, people adopt limiting beliefs about what they can accomplish; some even abandon their highest visions altogether.

However, with knowledge about human behavior and why people do what they do, individuals can develop a personalized strategy for changing their behavior so that it aligns with ultimate goals and values. This will allow them to take charge of their lives; effect real, lasting change; and improve the quality of their relationships, professional life, physical health, and emotional well being.

Awaken the Giant Within was published in 1992 by Summit Books and became an instant *New York Times* bestseller.

Important People

Tony Robbins is a strategist, entrepreneur, and self-help guru whose mission is to help people take control of their lives. He is a self-made multimillionaire and the author of several bestsellers including *Unlimited Power* (1986) and *Money: Master the Game* (2014).

Key Takeaways

1. The power of decision-making is the single most important factor in personal growth and transformation.

2. The three elements of significant personal change are raising standards, altering limiting beliefs, and adopting fresh strategies for action.

3. Two critical factors, the avoidance of pain and the quest for pleasure, motivate human behavior.

4. To change a negative behavior, people must learn to associate pain with that behavior instead of pleasure.

5. Events are neither good nor bad, but the meaning people ascribe to them will affect their emotional state for better or worse.

6. Change can happen instantly as long as there is a clear strategy and a willingness to question existing beliefs.

7. Personal responsibility is essential to growth and transformation.

8. People can utilize the power of their brains to effect lasting change by conditioning their nervous systems to react to certain behaviors.

9. People crave the feelings that they believe will come with certain achievements as opposed to the achievements themselves.

10. Well-crafted questions are key to directing change and achieving success in all areas of life.

11. People can learn to harness the power of their emotions, positive and negative, to direct their lives in a more productive and fulfilling way.

Thank you for purchasing this Instaread book

Download the Instaread mobile app to get unlimited text & audio summaries of bestselling books.

Visit Instaread.co to learn more.

Analysis

Key Takeaway 1

The power of decision-making is the single most important factor in personal growth and transformation.

Analysis

There's a difference between being interested in, say, losing weight, and committing to losing weight. If people are committed, they will take action. But before people take action, they must make a decision to commit to this goal. Then they can harness their own personal power and start to make incremental progress toward achieving it.

A-list actor Jim Carrey is a perfect illustration of how a single decision can direct a person's destiny. Carrey's father chose to become an accountant even though he was more passionate about having a career in comedy. His father reasoned that accounting was a safer route to economic security. When Carrey was 12, his father was laid off, and this turn of events had a huge impact on the budding actor. In a commencement address to Maharishi University of Management, he told graduates, "I learned a great many lessons from my father, not the least of which was that you can fail at what you don't want, so you might as well take a chance on doing what you love." Carrey made a decision to follow his heart instead of taking a seemingly safe route as his father believed he had. Following this decision, he achieved a great deal of success as the star of major motion pictures. [1]

Key Takeaway 2

The three elements of significant personal change are raising standards, altering limiting beliefs, and adopting fresh strategies for action.

Analysis

To enact real change, people first have to expect more of themselves and decide what it is they will no longer tolerate. Then, they must inspect their beliefs and choose only empowering ones so they can be confident that they can meet their new standards. Finally, they should choose strategic methods for achieving their goals.

To illustrate these principles, imagine a young, successful woman who is unhappy in her job as a private chef even though she makes a substantial salary and works for a prominent and kind family. She likes that her paycheck allows her to pay off her debts while affording her a luxurious lifestyle. But when she's cooking the same dinner for the hundredth time, she realizes that she needs to raise her own standards—she *is* capable of starting her own artisanal food line, a lifelong dream, but instead has settled into complacency in her cushy job.

Once she has decided that she won't settle for an unfulfilling job, she quickly identifies the biggest roadblock to striking out on her own: the naysaying voice in her head that tells her it's too scary to try something new because so-called vanity projects never make money. Since this belief doesn't gel with her decision to end the stagnant period in which she finds herself, she changes her thinking and tells herself, "I can absolutely find happiness *and* financial rewards in my new career path." Once she truly believes that she can make a leap, she sets out to learn from people who have achieved similar goals. She studies their methods. At this point, she doesn't need to know exactly how she will launch her line, but she has a firm foundation for enacting change and meeting her goal.

Key Takeaway 3

Two critical factors, the avoidance of pain and the quest for pleasure, motivate human behavior.

Analysis

When people are dissatisfied, they often examine external indicators of their unhappiness. Perhaps their body is out of shape or they are addicted to a high-stress job. Rarely do people examine the internal impulses that got them into a challenging situation. Once people realize that human behavior is driven by avoiding pain or seeking pleasure, they can view change in a new, empowering light.

This notion of pleasure versus pain has been explored by philosophers for thousands of years. Epicurus, a Greek philosopher who lived in the third century BC, wrote about this concept in *The Art of Happiness*. He wrote, "Not what we have but what we enjoy, constitutes our abundance." [2] He felt that happiness was, in fact, not a possession, but a lack: a lack of pain and sorrow. [3]

Key Takeaway 4

To change a negative behavior, people must learn to associate pain with that behavior instead of pleasure.

Analysis

Once people are aware of pleasure and pain instincts, they can make concrete progress toward changing bad behaviors by adopting new associative links. By the same token, people can also adopt a new positive attitude toward the positive behavior they want to embrace.

This optimistic approach is the basis for many self-help books including *The Game of Life and How to Play It* (1925), a classic in this genre by Florence Scovel Shinn. According to Shinn, the best way to win at life is to change one's expectations and thoughts to reflect positive outcomes. In a contrasting example, she relays the story of a man who feared a specific disease so intensely that he thought about it non-stop until he contracted it and died. In Shinn's view, if the man could have trained his "imagining faculty" to envision perfect health, he probably wouldn't have contracted the fatal disease. [4] He might instead have found more pleasure and health in retraining himself to focus on lighter or more constructive pursuits that improved his mental and physical health, and most of all his happiness.

Key Takeaway 5

Events are neither good nor bad, but the meaning people ascribe to them will affect their emotional state for better or worse.

Analysis

When people feel badly about a situation, it's because they have given negative meaning to it based on their beliefs. For example, a woman might believe that her boss only values her contributions when he says so explicitly. So when she works extra hard on a project and doesn't get instant affirmation, she sometimes thinks, "Oh, my boss doesn't think I did a worthy job." Her interpretation of this event would then create a negative feeling, when the reality could simply be that her boss was rushed and planned to follow up with her later. Instead of jumping to negative conclusions, coming up with more powerful and positive interpretations can generate an effective chain reaction by creating more positive feelings, which lead to more constructive action, which in turn brings people closer to their ultimate goals and destiny.

Philosophers and thinkers have opined about the human tendency to ascribe meaning to events. In *Feeling Good* (1980), psychologist David Burns writes that for people to have a feeling about a situation they must first understand it. Understanding, or interpretation, is acquired via rational thoughts. Thus, according to Burns, thoughts about situations and events always precede feelings about those same events. [5] If people's default is to interpret events more positively, they will naturally have more pleasant emotional experiences.

Key Takeaway 6

Change can happen instantly as long as there is a clear strategy and a willingness to question existing beliefs.

Analysis

Traditional psychologists believe that true personal transformation only comes through a laborious and lengthy process of introspection. Most people burden themselves with the belief that real change can't happen rapidly. This is false. Once people discard this limiting belief, they need only the right tools to support them to achieve their transformation, as well as a desire to push themselves out of their comfort zone.

The real-life example of author and entrepreneur Vishen Lakhiani illustrates just how rapidly change can happen if a person adopts a positive mindset. In 2008, Lakhiani realized that his company was losing $15,000 every month. In eight short months, he turned his company completely around and increased revenue by 400 percent. He did this using a technique he calls "bending reality," in which people balance their current happiness with their powerful future vision. [6] His route to becoming more successful and creating quick change came from his realization that he needed to have more fun in the moment while not losing sight of his ultimate goals.

Key Takeaway 7

Personal responsibility is essential to growth and transformation.

Analysis

While it's important to choose the right coach or therapist to assist one's journey to change, people need to be fully accountable for their own growth, development, and success. If a people believe that an outside party is the crucial catalyst of their change, the change won't last because they will always have someone else to blame if they relapse.

People often blame their problems on a difficult history. But past doesn't have to be prologue, especially when people become aware that they *can* gain mastery over their own lives. Media mogul Oprah Winfrey exemplifies this concept. In 2012, Oprah's Lifeclass featured the former talk show host explaining the moment she learned she had to take responsibility for her own life. At the age of six, she was taken from her grandmother, who was her primary source of care and love. This moment translated into a profound understanding of why it was critical to take charge of her life. Oprah says of this moment, "I have always had the deep understanding for myself that if anything was going to move forward in my life that I was going to have to be responsible for making that happen." [7] She urged her viewers to not wait idly by for someone else to fix their personal problems: "…only you have the power to…move your life forward. The sooner you get that, the sooner your life gets into gear." [8]

Key Takeaway 8

People can utilize the power of their brains to effect lasting change by conditioning their nervous systems to react to certain behaviors.

Analysis

Neurons, or cells that transmit nerve impulses, help human beings to interpret events; they convey critical information about how the nervous system is conditioned to react to various situations. People can examine their neuro-associations, that is, the pleasure and pain they link to certain behaviors or experiences, and then retrain their brain to have positive neuro-associations attached to desired behaviors.

Animal trainers have been using neuro-associations to condition animals for years, and their lessons have application for human behavior. Writer Amy Sutherland, for example, was working on a book about an exotic animal training school when she had an epiphany: the same lessons these trainers used could work on her husband's behavior. She'd been struggling in the marriage and was willing to try anything. So she positively reinforced behavior she desired, just as the trainers did with dolphins and elephants. For example, when her husband put his dirty shirts in the hamper instead of leaving them on the floor, she'd kiss him. When he didn't, she'd ignore him, an example of what the trainers called "least reinforcing syndrome" (LRS). This strategy worked, but in changing her husband's neuro-associations, she also changed her own. Her marriage improved because the process made her more loving and less judgmental. Sutherland realized that her husband was mirroring her positive reinforcement strategy and implementing a few LRS strategies of his own. [9]

Key Takeaway 9

People crave the feelings that they believe will come with certain achievements as opposed to the achievements themselves.

Analysis

Contrary to apparent logic, it's easy for people to achieve their goals and still feel emotionally unfulfilled. A rarely acknowledged truth is that people don't actually want the fancy job, flush bank account, or even the permanence of a 50-year marriage. What they *really* want is the happiness that they believe will accompany those things. Therefore, it's important to proactively create the feeling of happiness from within, and to experience it in the present, before and as goals are achieved. Once people master this skill, they are more likely to achieve their goals *and* feel good once they meet their goals.

Most people can relate to a feeling of anxiety or even disappointment after achieving a long-held goal. A dermatologist might spend three years developing a skin care line that reflects her values and passion for aesthetics, only to feel let down at the launch. A writer may toil for 10 years on a book and then feel empty after the publication date. In both of these cases, the individual forgot to be proactive about cultivating happiness along the way. Had they spent more time appreciating their good fortune and focusing on the joy of creation, they might not attach their happiness to the outcome and understand that they're already living their dream.

Key Takeaway 10

Well-crafted questions are key to directing change and achieving success in all areas of life.

Analysis

Questions are integral to personal transformation. They can be as empowering as, "What can I learn from this challenging situation?" Or they can be as disempowering as, "What's wrong with me that I can't snap out of this funk?" This latter inquiry will direct a person to think about negative factors or traits, whereas the former question implies that all experiences can be growth experiences. Choosing productive and positive questions is a skill that can be learned; it can steer a person's focus away from negative, destructive thoughts.

An empowering question can shape a person's subsequent experience and even their actions. For example, Karen Walsh, a Broadway actress and married mother of two, was diagnosed in 2015 with Stage IV colon cancer. Her health status threatened to overwhelm her well being as she struggled to come up with a concrete, practical way of handling her new reality. Instead of wallowing in a non-affirming question, such as, "What is the worst thing that can happen to me?", Walsh asked a better question: "What can I do to make this experience more positive?" Knowing that she didn't want to sit in a hospital room alone while she received her chemotherapy infusions, Walsh decided to ask her friends and family to accompany her. She came up with the idea to stage elaborate, light-hearted photo shoots, in which she and her loved ones would dress up as movie characters. [10] Not only did this help ensure that Walsh maintained a positive focus; it also resonated with many others who have endured chemo in isolation. The unexpected result for Walsh has been the gratification that others are benefiting from her difficult situation. [11] Knowing how to frame questions, as Walsh did, can greatly enrich the quality and satisfaction of change.

Key Takeaway 11

People can learn to harness the power of their emotions, positive and negative, to direct their lives in a more productive and fulfilling way.

Analysis

Instead of disavowing negative emotions or wallowing in them, people can view negative feelings as helpful signposts toward their next steps. For example, anger is an indicator that people feel their personal boundaries or rules have been violated. When anger is provoked, people can assess whether or not the offending party knew these rules and ask what they can learn from the situation. After this determination, they can decide to focus more on emotions that are empowering, such as love and curiosity.

Denying negative emotions might make a person feel inauthentic. Moreover, challenging emotions can actually enrich a person's life. Psychologist Jonathan Adler of the Franklin W. Olin College of Engineering says, "Acknowledging the complexity of life may be an especially fruitful path to psychological well-being…Remember, one of the primary reasons we have emotions in the first place is to help us evaluate our experiences." [12] Therefore, it's important for people to embrace a range of emotions so that they can channel their feelings in a way that propels them toward their ultimate destiny.

Author's Style

Tony Robbins writes in an engaging, motivating style. He uses many real-life stories including tales of triumph from people who have attended his workshops and from well-known public figures including Bill Gates, George Bush, and Gandhi. He also uses his own life experience to fully explain his personal transformation principles and strategy for success. He breaks down his thought process and how he came to certain conclusions. For example, when a man he helped to quit smoking started again, he realized that he had been taking full responsibility for the man's changed behavior. This made him realize how important it is for individuals to take full responsibility for their choices, but it also helped Robbins evolve his vision of how to help people. He outlines the methods that he uses for rapid change including neuro-linguistic programming, a method by which shifts in language produce new neurological associations that lead to different behaviors and feelings. He is specific about the role of language in transformation and writes at length about how certain words and metaphors can change the tenor of a person's mood or interpersonal relationships and how being language-conscious has an ultimate result of being a more effective person overall.

Robbins writes in a clear and methodical format. He repeats his ideas throughout the book and makes associations whenever relevant. Robbins directly challenges the readers to read the whole book and also do certain exercises right as they are reading, such as a 10-day challenge of not complaining. He includes a comprehensive index of topics, as well as information on the Anthony Robbins Foundation, in case readers want to get involved.

Author's Perspective

Tony Robbins became a self-made millionaire at the age of 24 after suffering many setbacks and challenges including an unstable childhood. His own life experience has caused him to be passionate about principles of change. He views helping others to achieve their goals as his life's calling. In 1991, he founded the Anthony Robbins Foundation, which supports education and other social welfare causes. Robbins is well-aware of how he can positively impact others and gains great satisfaction from being of service to people who wish to change their lives in ways large and small.

~~~~ END OF INSTAREAD ~~~~

Thank you for purchasing this Instaread book

Download the Instaread mobile app to get unlimited text & audio summaries of bestselling books.

Visit Instaread.co to learn more.

References

1. Westerholm, Russell. "Jim Carrey Talks on Decision Making and Meditation in Commencement Address at Maharishi University of Management." *University Herald Reporter.* May 28, 2014. Accessed September 2, 2016. http://www.universityherald.com/articles/9651/20140528/jim-carrey-talks-on-decision-making-and-meditation-in-commencement-address-at-maharishi-university-of-management-video.htm

2. Epicurus. *The Art of Happiness.* New York: Penguin Classics, 2012, p. viii.

3. Ibid., p. ix.

4. Shinn, Florence Scovel. *The Game of Life and How to Play It.* New York: Merchant Books, 2013, p. 7.

5. Burns, David. *Feeling Good: The New Mood Therapy.* New York: Avon, 1980, 1999, loc. 657.

6. Lakhiani, Vishen. *The Code of the Extraordinary Mind: 10 Unconventional Laws to Redefine Your Life & Succeed on Your Own Terms.* New York: Rodale Books, 2016, pp. 116-118.

7. Winfrey, Oprah. "'Be Responsible for Your Own Life,' Says Oprah." *The Huffington Post.* December

31, 2012. Accessed September 2, 2016. http://www.huffingtonpost.com/2012/12/31/be-responsible-take-responsibility-oprah_n_2330820.html

8. Ibid.

9. Sutherland, Amy. "What Shamu Taught Me About a Happy Marriage." *The New York Times*. June 25, 2006. Accessed September 2, 2016. http://www.nytimes.com/2006/06/25/fashion/25love.html

10. Prakash, Alesha. "Cancer patient transforms chemo into must-see photo shoot." *The Today Show*. July 15, 2016. Accessed September 2, 2016. http://www.today.com/health/cancer-patient-transforms-chemo-must-see-photo-shoot-t100852

11. Ibid.

12. Rodriguez, Tori. "Negative Emotions Are Key to Well-Being." *Scientific American*. May 1, 2013. Accessed September 12, 2016. http://www.scientificamerican.com/article/negative-emotions-key-well-being/

Lightning Source UK Ltd.
Milton Keynes UK
UKHW022254170120
357165UK00014B/234